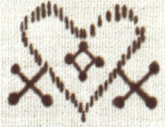

Stitching Freedom
Embroidery & Incarceration

By Isabella Rosner

First published in 2024 by Common Threads Press

ISBN: 978-1-91632-347-6

Edited by Eleanor Gaffney and Laura Moseley
Illustrations by Takako Copeland
Design by Chris Shortt
Typeset in Zarathustra (Lorène Picard) and Selectric Century (Jens Kutilek)
Printed and bound by Short Run Press, Exeter, Devon, UK

© Common Threads Press, 2024

All rights reserved. Contributions have been commissioned and therefore no part of this publication may be reproduced or copied in any form or by any means without permission of the copyright owners. Exceptions include the artists and authors sharing their own work, brief quotations, reviews and certain other non-commercial uses permitted by copyright law. The right of Isabella Rosner to be identified as author of this work has been asserted in accordance with Section 77 of the Copyright, Designs and Patents Act of 1988.

Stitching Freedom

By Isabella Rosner

Common Threads Press

Introduction	07
Virtue Flourishes by Wounding	11
In Lonely Grief I Sigh	15
Damnation Hell Tramp Den of Old Women	19
I Plunge Headlong Into Disaster	25
Bold Bad Ones	31
Filled With My Love Always	36

Fuck Hitler

Codemakers, Codebreakers

Many Innocents Have Perished

Becoming God

The Mystery of Myrllen

Betsy Ross

Conclusion

INTRODUCTION

Embroidery has long been considered a gentle, docile, polite craft practised by women of leisure. But to understand embroidery as an art for just the privileged few is to minimise embroidery's importance to thousands of individuals from all over the world, in a wide range of circumstances. Though in the past embroidery was more often undertaken by women, it was and continues to be an activity for people of all genders, races, religions, sexualities, socioeconomic statuses and locations. Schoolgirl samplers of the past and embroidery kits of the present are just the tip of the iceberg.

People have always stitched in good times and in bad. For centuries, individuals embroidered in hard times and under difficult circumstances, finding freedom in the calming repetition of a needle moving in and out of fabric. Some of those people undertook this needlework in prisons and psychiatric institutions, expressing their anguish and their ambitions through stitch.

This book focuses on embroidery stitched in prisons and mental health hospitals in order to bring out these often forgotten stories and to illustrate that embroidery is more than an elegant pastime. The story of incarceration and embroidery in the face of distress is much bigger than can fit on the pages of this book, but these tales are representative of other people who embroidered in prisons and hospitals, such as Mary Frances Heaton, Gabriele Urbach and Jane Grier. There is the embroidery of Indian, African and Native American girls in nineteenth-century British and American missionary schools, coerced into conforming to Europeanised ideas of Christianity and womanhood. There is also Elizabeth Parker, whose stitched sampler in the collection of the Victoria and Albert Museum relays her despair and poor treatment at the hands of her employers; and the convict stitchers of the Rajah Quilt, who crafted a patchworked and embroidered quilt while on the journey to Britain's penal colony in Australia.

Embroidered stories from prisons and mental health facilities coexist in this book. Though prisons and hospitals differ greatly, those who are in them often experience shared feelings and face some of the same restrictions. In both institutions, the power rests with the institution rather than the individual, resulting in emotions like anger, sadness and confusion. As will be seen again and again in these stories, stitching materials did not come easily to incarcerated embroiderers, who often had to scavenge for sewing needles and embroidery thread. It makes sense, then, that the art made in these places share common themes. The following pages are an exercise in discovering what can be created in spaces where freedom is out of reach.

The twelve individuals or groups discussed here are stitched together by a shared art form. But why did they all seek out embroidery? Perhaps it was a way to be creative, to pass the time, to express emotions, to calm down, to distract, to reflect, to rehabilitate, or even to enact violence upon fabric with a needle. Embroidery can embody contradiction, with each stitch simultaneously perpetuating rage and inspiring calm. ●

CONTENT WARNING
Please note: some of the stories here involve suicide, violence, abuse and death.

Virtue Flourishes by Wounding

455 years ago, a queen embroidered a picture of her dog. The dog is white with two black spots, slightly resembling a cow. The dog's name is Jupiter. The queen's name is Mary, Queen of Scots (1542–1587).

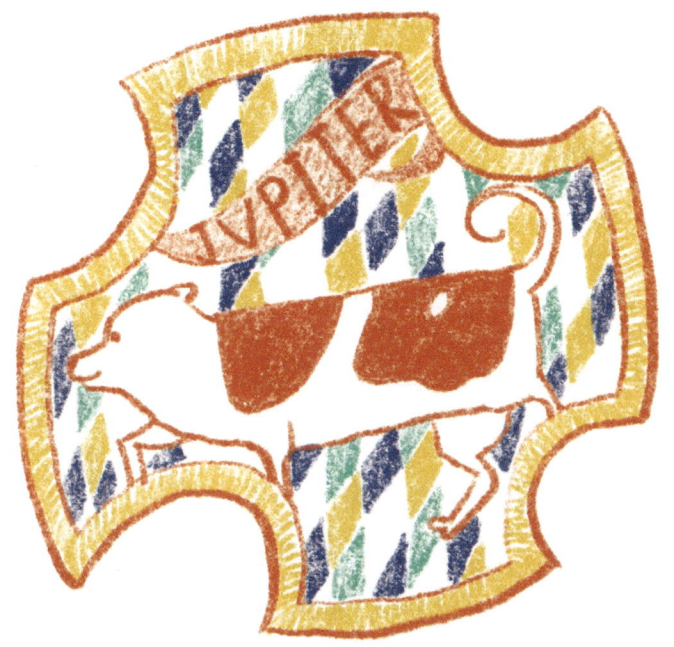

Mary, Queen of Scots has given us the earliest surviving example of incarceration embroidery. The Catholic queen fled Scotland in May 1568, attempting to leave behind months of turmoil which ended in her forced abdication and imprisonment in Loch Leven Castle. She escaped and headed towards England, where she believed her cousin, Queen Elizabeth I, would help her regain her throne. Instead, Elizabeth had Mary imprisoned for almost nineteen years, culminating in Mary's execution in 1587.

Mary was imprisoned in the various properties of the Earl of Shrewsbury and his wife, Bess of Hardwick, who were assigned to be Mary's jailers. Under house arrest, Mary was afforded more privileges than her counterparts in this book's eleven other stories; she had her own staff, access to some material luxuries and the ability to receive visitors. Though Mary was not locked behind prison bars, she was constantly surveilled by the Earl and Countess, her letters were censored and her outdoor activity was limited. A lack of exercise meant that she developed rheumatism and was always in pain.

As she had done throughout her life, Mary turned to stitch. Embroidery became a helpful distraction, allowing her to express feelings she could not through the written word. She found herself in good company, as Bess of Hardwick was also a keen needleworker. Together they created a series of tent and cross-stitched slips — embroideries worked on linen or canvas that are cut out and applied to larger, oftentimes finer fabrics like velvet or silk. Mary, Queen of Scots's handiwork is now in the collection of the Victoria and Albert Museum and the Royal Collection Trust.

Mary took inspiration for her embroideries from the emblem books that were so popular in the period, as well as botanical and natural history books. Some of her scenes are illustrations of Aesop's fables. With stitch she presents us details from her life, such as the depiction of her dog Jupiter and images from the literature she had access to. She illustrates moments from her past and from her present. My favourite is an embroidery in which a ginger cat wearing a crown on its head observes a small grey mouse scurrying by. In the scene, which Mary titles 'A CATTE' (a factual title that nevertheless makes me giggle), the orange cat is Elizabeth and the fearful mouse is Mary herself. In another piece, she shows a fashionably dressed wrist and hand descending from the sky, holding a pruning knife to a grapevine. Above this is a Latin verse, **VIRESCIT VULNERE VIRTUE**, meaning 'virtue flourishes by wounding'. With this, Mary stakes her claim to the throne, suggesting that Elizabeth's fruitless branch of the Tudor tree should be cut away. Though Mary's embroideries seemed innocent, they were rife with code.

Just as the content of Mary's embroideries illustrated distress, frustration and anger, so did her stitching. From a distance, Mary's embroidery is uniform, but a closer glance reveals it to be a bit chaotic, with stitches every so often uneven or missing altogether. This is the embroidery of a woman who started a queen and ended a prisoner, who used stitch as a means of seeking solace and expressing her anguish. •

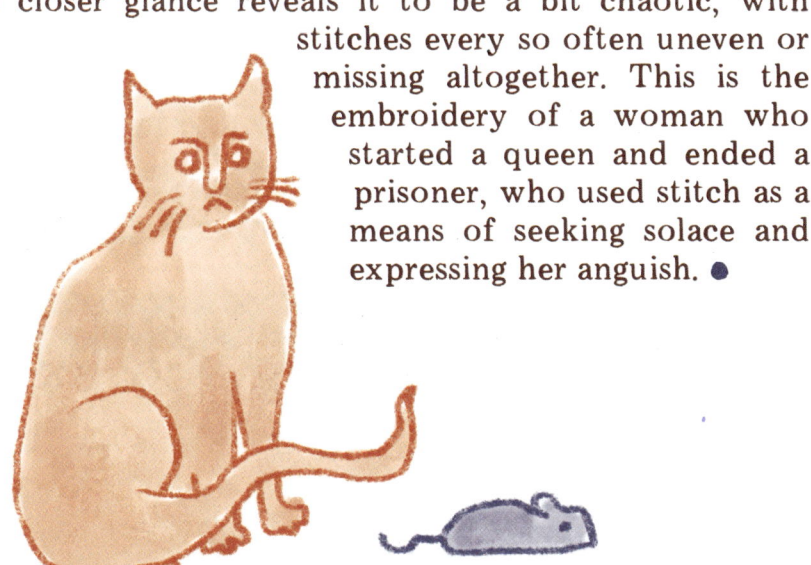

In Lonely Grief

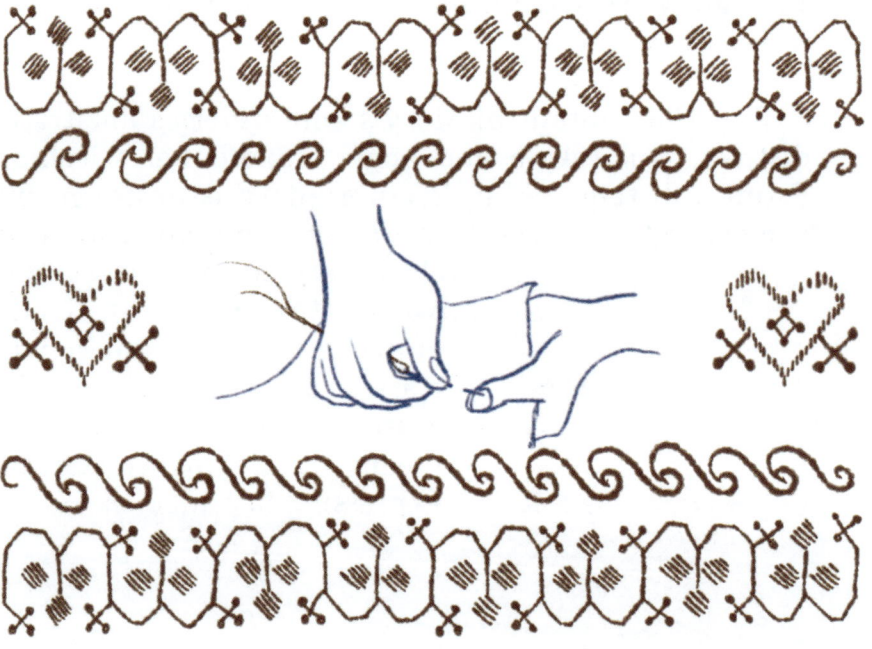

I Sigh

In its best moments, embroidery has offered those in prisons and asylums a mental and physical escape, a sense of control and calm, and even agency. It has also given them a chance to express and make a permanent mark of their desperation. One of those incarcerated stitchers, a Londoner named Annie Parker (c.1847–1885), was so desperate that she made that mark with her body. She embroidered pincushions and samplers, using her own hair as thread.

In March 1879, Annie Parker was convicted of drunkenness and sentenced to one month of imprisonment with hard labour. At that point in 1879, she had spent 350 of the past 365 days in prison. By her death at 38 years old in 1885, Parker had been arrested over 400 times. Very little is known about Parker's origins — we know she was born in 1847 or 1848 and was well educated, but we do not know where or by who. This may be the same Annie Parker who, according to an 1877 newspaper article, was first arrested for drunkenness in 1859. In that article, they incorrectly give her age as 40; in reality, she was 29 or 30, making her 11 or 12 years old when she was jailed for the first time. How she ended up in this position remains a mystery. At one point, Annie was 'rescued' by the Church of England Temperance Society, who found her lodgings with a well-meaning woman. Parker ran away, returning to life in the workhouse, where she spent much of her time when not in prison. She died in the Greenwich workhouse infirmary of consumption.

During her many years in prison, she stitched objects with religious verses and gave them to employees at the prisons and detention centres she landed in.

Several of Parker's hairwork embroideries survive — they are in the National Justice Museum, Museum of London and private collections. They are relics of a woman with an addiction who lived in a world that was not equipped to help her.

When she died in August of 1885, *Reynolds's Newspaper* memorialised Parker's hair and schooling: 'SHE HAD A LUXURIANT HEAD OF HAIR' and not only was she 'ALWAYS EXCEEDINGLY WELL CONDUCTED IN PRISON', she 'HAD RECEIVED AN EXCELLENT EDUCATION'. These comments perfectly encapsulate how embroidery was tied to morality in the Victorian era. In her life and immediately after it, Parker was mythologised. She was treated as a spectacle who embodied everything a proper Victorian should and should not be: she was well-educated, pious and well-mannered, but also uncontrollable and unvirtuous.

It is not clear how Parker got fabric and a needle. Perhaps like other stories in this book, she was given a needle and bleached linen by a sympathetic prison guard. Did she pluck her hair because she was not given thread or had no textiles on hand to unravel? Maybe yes, or maybe it was a way to garner sympathy from the members of the Greenwich penal system, men who had known her in the courtroom and the prison since 1859 and who had the power to lessen her prison sentences. This may have worked, given that she was never convicted of a felony. Or maybe it was a form of reflection and punishment, a way to reprimand herself for her addiction and attempt to heal herself through pious verse and orderly stitches. The rhyming verses she embroidered reflect this:

Though dark my path and sad my lot
Let me be still and murmur not

[...]

What though in lonely grief I sigh
For friends beloved no longer nigh

[...]

Renew my will from day to day
Blend it with thine and take away
All that now makes it hard to say
Thy will be done

Annie clearly battled demons in the prison cell and beyond, with published reports stating that she tore up her clothes and attempted suicide. The turmoil of her daily life is translated into desperation and deep sorrow in her stitching. The fact that she used her own head of 'luxuriant' hair to embroider her suffering shows more than resourcefulness: it shows someone using her own body to try to mend her mind. Not only that, it exhibits a woman using Victorian modes of needlework to stitch herself back into the world outside of the penal state. ●

Damnation Hell Tramp Den of Old Women

In the 21st century, sometimes being angry means typing a tweet, an Instagram or Facebook comment, a text, or an email in all-caps. It is an understandable tendency to yell with the written word and spew it across the Internet at a stranger, a business, or simply into the ether. Now imagine writing that uppercase, grammarless diatribe in stitch. And imagine that rant being 16 feet long. Enter Lorina Bulwer's embroidered rants, now in the collection of the Norwich Castle Museum and Thackray Museum of Medicine.

When Lorina Bulwer (1838–1912) was 55 years old, she was sent to the Great Yarmouth Workhouse in Norfolk, England. Bulwer seems to have grown up middle-class and well-educated, the daughter of parents who owned a chain of grocery stores in Great Yarmouth. She never married. Instead, she ran a guest house for 22 years between the deaths of her father and mother. When her mother died in 1893, her brother Edgar sent her to the workhouse and paid for her to be kept there. He considered his 55-year-old sister to be incapable of running her own affairs.

When Bulwer entered the Great Yarmouth Workhouse, it was home to approximately 500 inmates, about 60 of whom were determined to be mentally ill and classified as 'lunatics'. Bulwer was included in this group. Bulwer and her peers said to be 'lunatics' were made to unpick oakum (fibres that come from untwisting old rope) for up to ten hours a day. Bulwer lived at the workhouse for the rest of her life, a total of 19 years.

In the little free time she had, Bulwer stitched. She embroidered with fury, with frustration. She was furious she was in the workhouse and she wanted you to know. She pieced together strips of cotton and embroidered upon them with wool threads. Where did she get that fabric and those threads? It is difficult to say, but, if she was anything like the other institutionalised embroiderers in this book, she took her fabric from discarded hospital sheets or uniforms and her threads from unravelled garments.

Bulwer's all-caps rants, spread across three 'samplers' (called such because they are similar in composition to contemporary samplers), are a mixture of reality and fiction. The shortest piece is 12 feet long and the longest 15.8 feet long. She mentions over 70 people in her stitching but not all of them are those she knew personally. The royal family, who she never met, is an example:

I AM PRINCESS VICTORIA'S DAUGHTER LORINA BULWER WAS TAKEN TO THE ROYAL NUSERY [sic] QUEEN VICTORIAS [sic] IN HER INFANCY

Bulwer describes people, cracks jokes, shares gossip and makes accusations. She hints at sexual abuse at the hands of Dr Richard Lloyd Pinching of Walthamstow, stitching:

> I MISS LORINA BULWER WAS EXAMINED BY DR PINCHING OF WALTHAMSTOW ESSEX AND FOUND TO BE A PROPERLY SHAPED FEMALE

Dr Pinching was implicated in the sexual abuse of a 14-year-old girl in 1859. Her feelings about her institutionalisation can be summarised in her stitched scream:

> I HAVE WASTED TEN YEARS IN THS [sic] DAMNATION HELL TRAMP DEN OF OLD WOMEN OLD BAGS

There are lots of questions about how and why Bulwer was allowed to embroider such angry diatribes aimed at specific and sometimes high-ranking individuals. Perhaps it was a way to keep her occupied or was viewed as a form of therapy. Maybe no one cared or maybe someone saw its artistic value.

Like so many of the objects in this book, the unfortunate answer to these questions is 'Who knows?' Even though Bulwer screams, we cannot fully understand. What we can comprehend, though, is how different Bulwer's stitching was from that of her contemporaries. Bulwer's embroidery stands in stark contrast to the delicacy and naturalism of the art needlework in which many of her fellow turn-of-the-twentieth-century Englishwomen were invested. From their needles grew delicate floral motifs, but from Lorina Bulwer's needle erupted furor and violence. This was not a needle innocently winding its way in and out of cloth, but a knife producing verbal bloodshed with every stab of the fabric. She was raging against her family, her history and the world in which she lived. In a world that makes us angry, we feel seen by Lorina Bulwer's tirades. We, too, want to wail. ●

I HAVE
WASTED TEN
YEARS IN THS
DAMNATION
HELL
TRAMP DEN
OF OLD
WOMEN
OLD BAGS

I Plunge

Headlong

Into
Disaster

Here is a tiny jacket stitched with layer upon layer of embroidery. There is so much text on it that it is hard to make out every word, but if you look hard enough you can read some phrases in an old German script called *deutsche Schrift*. Emerging from the tangled stitches are sentences like, 'I WISH TO READ' and 'I PLUNGE HEADLONG INTO DISASTER'.

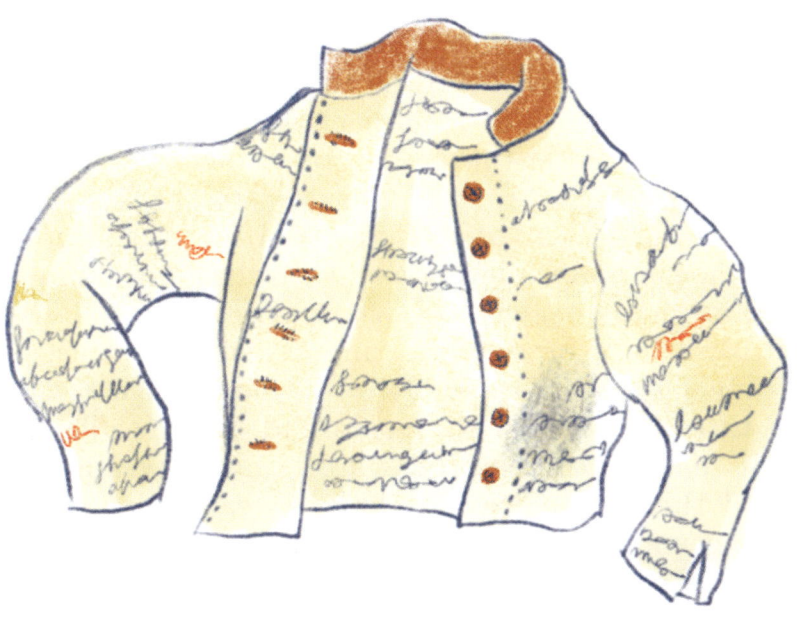

In 1893, a 49-year-old Dresden resident named Agnes Richter (1844–1918) was arrested. She was a small, stooped seamstress who had returned to Germany after eight years in the US. In America she amassed a small fortune and once she returned to Dresden she grew afraid that she would be robbed. Her fear led her to contact the police often. They arrested her for disturbing the peace and trespassing, which in turn led to a diagnosis of paranoia and an admission to the Dresden City Lunatic Asylum in 1893 and the Hubertusburg Asylum in 1895, where she remained for the last 23 years of her life.

It's not clear why Richter ended up in a psychiatric hospital. Some sources claim it was her father and brothers who had her admitted, while others say it was her neighbours. Or maybe it was none of those — perhaps she was admitted after being charged for trespassing. It is also not clear why Richter was moved from Dresden to Hubertusburg, more than 40 miles away, in 1895. What is clear though is that Richter did not enter the asylum by choice.

During the first year of her stay at Hubertusburg, Richter began embroidering a small jacket, one that she clearly made herself to fit her petite frame. The jacket is made of brown wool and coarse linen with embroidery stitched in red, yellow, blue, orange and white threads on both its inside and outside. The jacket's seams are facing outwards, the sleeves are attached the wrong way, and the sweat stains on the lining and shoulder seams don't match up. All of these clues point to Richter turning the jacket's torso inside out at some later point. Once one side of her jacket was laden with embroidery, she gave herself a new canvas upon which to stitch. Is it too bold to say that through the unmaking and remaking of this jacket Richter worked to stitch her life back together?

Housed in the Prinzhorn Collection since the early twentieth century, the jacket only became well known after being exhibited in 1980. Psychiatrist and art historian Hans Prinzhorn, for whom the Prinzhorn Collection is named, obtained the jacket for his collection of art by mentally ill individuals after Agnes Richter's death in 1919. Between 1919 and 1921, Prinzhorn, assistant psychiatrist at the psychiatric hospital of Heidelberg University, and Karl Willmanns, the head of the hospital, sent letters to psychiatric hospitals in German-speaking countries, asking for their patients' artworks. It is likely that Richter's jacket was sent to Prinzhorn by Hubertusburg staff. Prinzhorn's collection included thousands of objects, which he published in his 1922 book *Bildnerei der Geisteskranken: Ein Beitrag zur Psychologie und Psychopatologie der Gestaltung*, translated into English as 'ARTISTRY OF THE MENTALLY ILL: A CONTRIBUTION TO THE PSYCHOLOGY AND PSYCHOPATHOLOGY OF CONFIGURATION'. Prinzhorn died in 1933 and in 1938, some pieces from his collection were put on display in a Nazi exhibition called *Entartete Kunst* ('Degenerate Art'), where the art of the psychiatric patients was exploited to assert that modern art was the result of mental illness. The collection was largely forgotten about after World War II until it was rediscovered in 1963, and was later moved into an official museum in a formal lecture hall in Heidelberg University in 2001. Though Hans Prinzhorn seems to have largely ignored Agnes Richter's jacket and the artworks of other female patients, excluding many of them from his book, it has been the subject of much curiosity and scholarship over the last four decades.

A note attached to the jacket, likely written by the Hubertusburg employee who sent the jacket to Hans

Prinzhorn, translates to:

> Agnes Richter, 1895. Dem[entia] praec[ox]. Sewed reminiscences from her life into all of her undergarments and clothing.

The employee catalogued the item using the outdated term 'dementia praecox', which was eventually replaced by 'schizophrenia'. The rest of the label indicates that Richter embroidered on all of her clothing, but this jacket is the only piece that survives. Richter embroidered her jacket with *deutsche Schrift*, also known as *Kurrent*, an antiquated form of German cursive.

Most of the jacket's embroidery is illegible. Text is layered in many places and worn away in others. But some phrases can still be deciphered. Accompanying hopes like 'I WISH TO READ' and poignant reflections such as 'I PLUNGE HEADLONG INTO DISASTER' are statements of fact, such as 'MY JACKET' and 'I AM IN HUBERTUSBURG'. Other snippets of text are glimpses into longer trains of thought: 'NO CHERRIES' and 'BROTHER FREEDOM'.

It's easy to envision the embroiderers discussed here bent over their needlework, their shoulders and hands sore and their eyes aching. The curve of Agnes Richter's jacket makes that even more apparent, a physical sign of the contortion of stitch. For the women and men discussed here, embroidery grew from physical and emotional exertion. ●

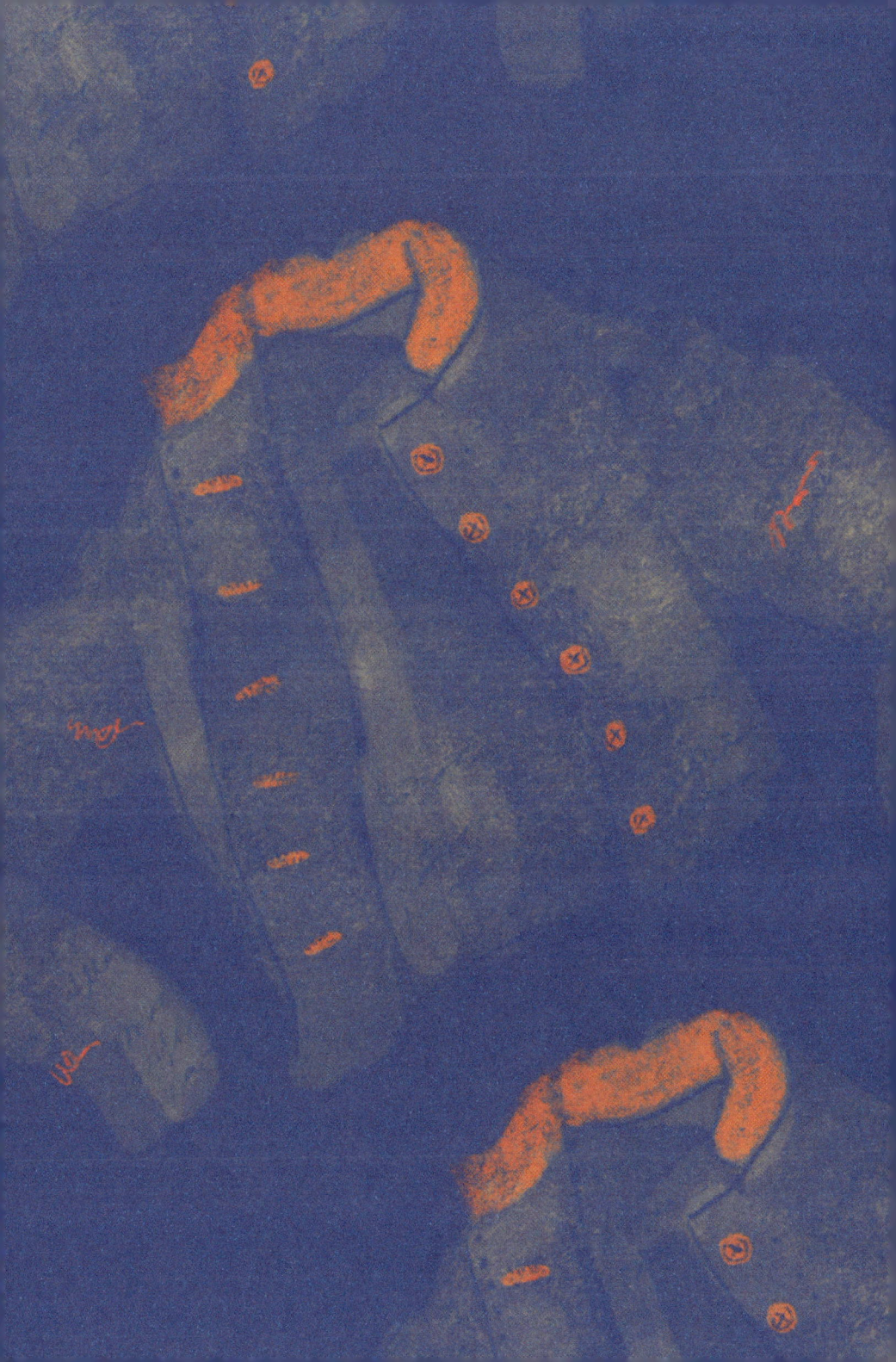

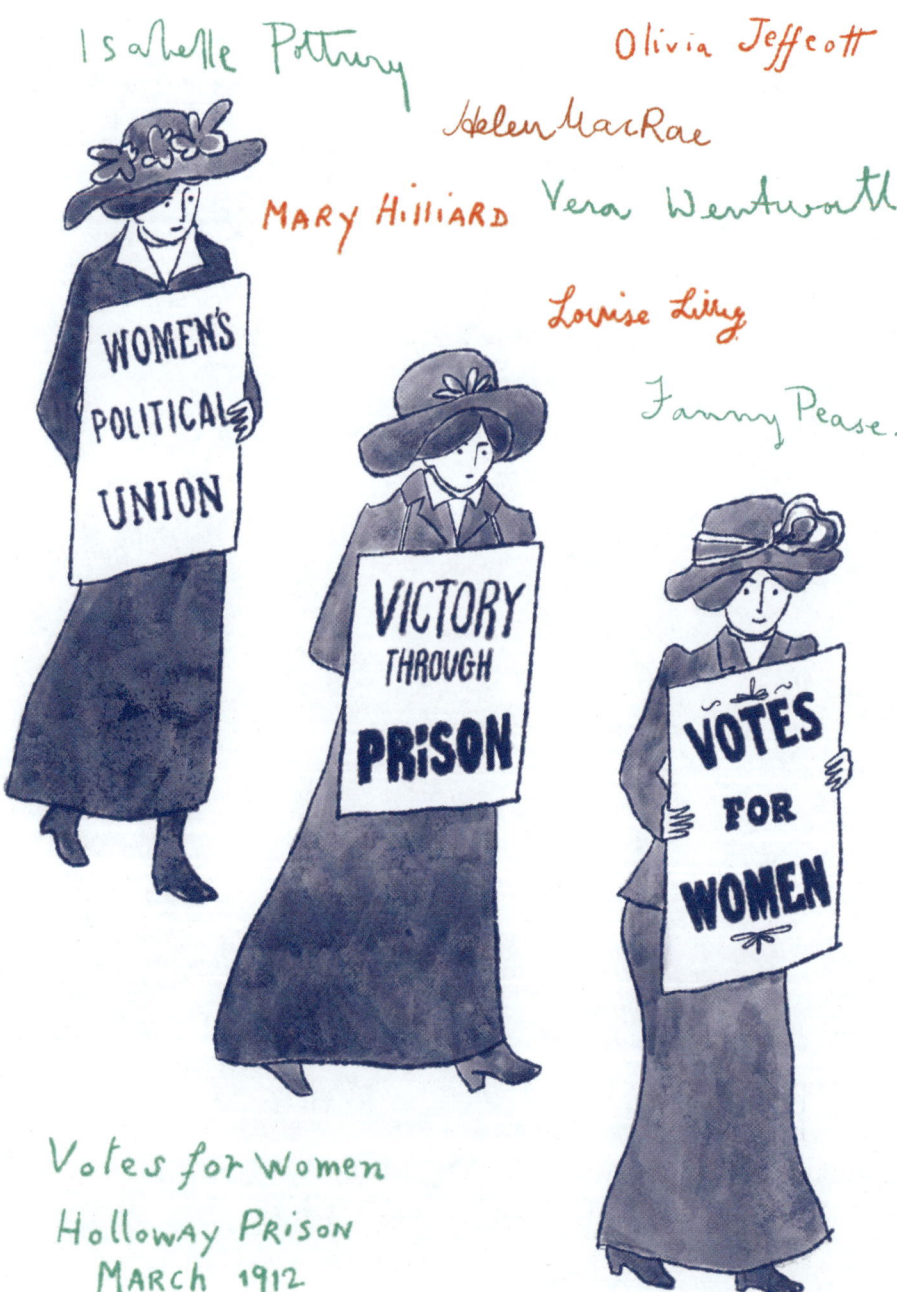

Bold Bad Ones

Several of the objects discussed in this book were found by accident, trapped under piles of abandoned fabrics and discovered languishing in attics or basements. In the 1970s, an embroidered handkerchief was up for sale at a jumble sale in West Hoathly, West Sussex. No one bought it so it was thrown onto a pile of textiles to be burnt. Someone (we do not know who) took it out of the pile (we do not know why), saving it from the conflagration. This abandoned handkerchief, now called 'The Suffragette Handkerchief', is embroidered with 66 signatures and two sets of initials belonging to women imprisoned in Holloway Prison for their participation in the March 1912 Women's Social and Political Union (WSPU) window-smashing demonstrations. This handkerchief — a souvenir started by Irish suffragette Mary Ann Hilliard and now in the collection of The Priest House — is part of a larger group of embroideries stitched by imprisoned suffragettes in the early 20th century.

Hilliard started the handkerchief as a souvenir to remember her fellow prisoners, all of whom were fighting to achieve votes for women. Some of those prisoners were hunger-strikers and some were force-fed. Some had been arrested previously and others were arrested again later. The white linen handkerchief is covered in embroidered signatures in a variety of colours, predominantly purple. Needles and threads were available to the female needleworkers. What resulted is an embroidered album, a stitched memento of suffering for a shared cause.

Hilliard's handkerchief fits within a larger landscape of suffragette prison stitching. Examples include but are not limited to another handkerchief stitched by Cissie Wilcox in 1912 (in the Museum of London, hereafter called MoL), a small sampler and bag stitched by Mary Aldham in Holloway Prison sometime between 1910 and 1914 (in a private collection), a shield badge embroidered with 'ASC' (MoL), a small bag embroidered with 'Grace' (MoL), another bag worked by Mary Ellen Taylor (The Women's Library), and a panel by Janie Terrero (MoL). With the exception of Aldham's pieces, all of the suffragette embroideries listed here are embroidered with the year 1912. Several of them are adorned with groups of stitched signatures. Some of the embroidered objects like bags and badges were made to be used and may have been given as gifts between fellow suffragettes.

Perhaps the best known is Janie Terrero's panel, which was long on display in the MoL's permanent galleries. Her panel is worked on wool in the typical WSPU colours of green, white and purple. An embroidered inscription in the middle includes the WSPU's motto of 'Deeds Not Words' and the description 'Worked in Holloway Prison by Janie Terrero'. Terrero's central text is flanked by lines of signatures, below which Terrero stitched 'Mrs. Pankhursts Bold Bad Ones' (Emmeline Pankhurst was the founder of the WSPU). The prevalence of signatures on these prison embroideries suggests these 'bold, bad' suffragettes viewed themselves as a community, each member an essential part of the whole.

These imprisoned women stitched to document their making of history. Denise Jones, in her PhD thesis 'Embroidering and the Body Under Threat: Suffragette Embroidered Cloths Worked in Holloway Prison, 1911—1912', shares that Mary Ellen Taylor wrote to her children while in jail: 'I might be able to do some fancy work. I could do a bit of work for each of you. When the Vote is won you might like to keep it in memory of this fight.' Unlike the banners suffragettes made for public display, the suffragette prison embroideries were personal. They were mementos not only of a fight well fought, but also of the women who battled and the actions they undertook to secure their victory.

These suffragettes enacted violence to fight for enfranchisement and were the victims of violence during the imprisonments that followed. In the prison, the stones used to destroy shop windows were exchanged for embroidery needles — their capacity for physical violence and damage different, but their emotional impact the same. ●

Filled With My Love

Always

My great grandmother Rose
mother of Ashley gave her this sack when
she was sold at age 9 in South Carolina
it held a tattered dress 3 handfulls of
pecans a braid of Roses hair Told her

It be filled with my Love always

she never saw her again

Ashley is my grandmother

Ruth Middleton

1921

Unlike prisons and hospitals, very little needlework produced by those who were victims of the institution of slavery survives. Those who were enslaved in America surely stitched, but their stitching was likely practical rather than decorative. Perhaps some enslaved people were made to undertake decorative stitching for those who enslaved them, and maybe a few of the enslaved were able to stitch for pleasure in rare moments. Our knowledge of what needlework enslaved individuals undertook is minimal because their objects so rarely survive with associated names and identities attached. It is likely that much more of their work survives than expected, but we do not know it is the work of enslaved individuals because it has been passed off as the work of white women. An exceptional embroidered object, called *Ashley's Sack*, tells the story of slavery in America and the love and care it attempted to destroy but could not. The bag was assembled while slavery in the US ran rampant; its embroidery was added approximately 70 years later, in its aftermath.

Ashley's Sack, in the collection of Middleton Place (but on loan to the International African American Museum), is a white cotton bag dating to around 1850. It was machine sewn, likely used to hold flour, seeds, or other food staples. It has been carefully patched in several areas. On the bag is an embroidered inscription in cursive, stitched in cotton thread, which reads:

> My great grandmother Rose
> mother of Ashley gave her this sack when
> she was sold at age 9 in South Carolina
> it held a tattered dress 3 handfulls of

      pecans a braid of Roses hair. Told her
          It be filled with my Love always
               she never saw her again
              Ashley is my grandmother
                    Ruth Middleton
                         1921

The inscription begins in brown thread and ends in green thread. The line 'It be filled with my Love always' is the only one in red and is separated from the rest of the text. 'Love' is the biggest word of all. Ironically, the power of family, connection and devotion in the face of slavery is illustrated through an object made from a slave-grown cotton textile.

The rediscovery of *Ashley's Sack* shares similarities with that of the Suffragette Handkerchief. In 2007, a woman found the sack in a bin of old fabric at a flea market. She connected the name Ruth Middleton to Middleton Place in South Carolina and gave it to the museum in exchange for a lifetime membership and a small amount of money. It was a curator at Middleton Place, Mary Edna Sullivan, who gave the object its name. Ruth Middleton did not have a connection to Middleton Place. Her great-grandmother, Rose, and her grandmother, Ashley, were enslaved by Robert Martin of South Carolina. According to Tiya Miles — whose book ALL THAT SHE CARRIED: THE JOURNEY OF ASHLEY'S SACK, A BLACK FAMILY KEEPSAKE is a thorough exploration of *Ashley's Sack* and the women connected to it — Ashley may have been sold away from her mother after Martin's death in 1852. Like Rose and Ashley, Ruth Middleton was from South Carolina. She moved to Philadelphia around 1918 and it is likely there that she stitched upon her grandmother's bag.

With her stitching, Middleton memorialised her ancestors' bravery, their love, their sacrifice and their trauma. Because of her stitching we know about Rose, Ashley and the precious gifts mother gave daughter before their parting. Through her embroidery we see a lineage of Black women's resistance and action. ●

My great grandmother
Rose mother of Ashley
gave her this sack when
she was sold at age 9
in South Carolina it
held a tattered dress 3
handfulls of pecans a
braid of Roses hair. Told
her It be filled with my
Love always she never
saw her again Ashley
is my grandmother
Ruth Middleton 1921

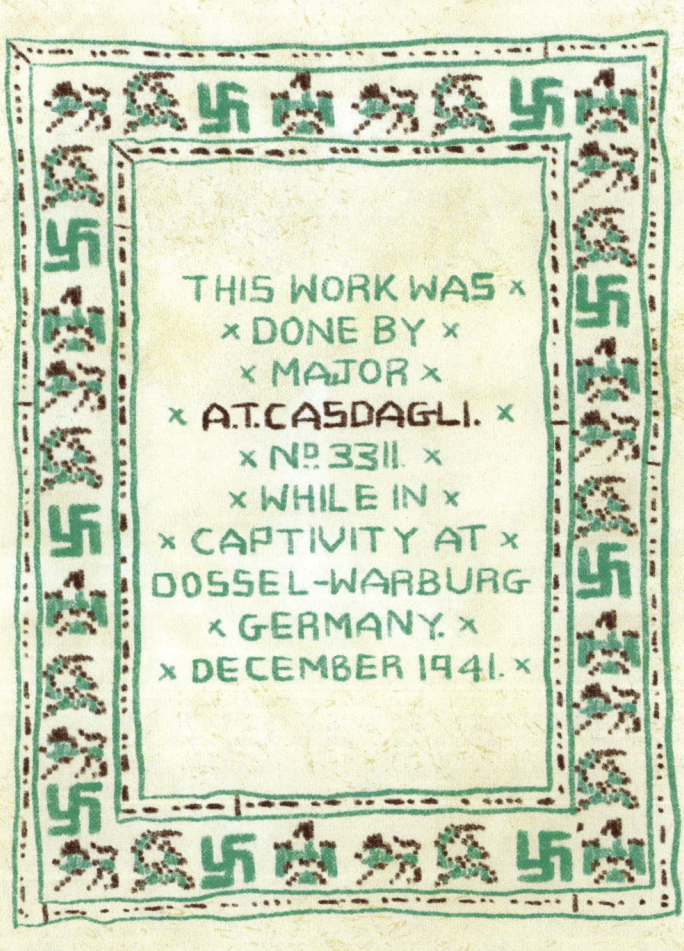

Fuck Hitler

It was cold in the Oflag IV-B camp in Dössel-Warburg, Germany in December 1941. Major Alexis Casdagli (1906–1996), a British army officer, found himself in the World War II prisoner-of-war camp that winter after being captured in Crete in June. One of his fellow prisoners gave him a piece of canvas. Another, a Cretan general, found himself exposed to winter's chill when Casdagli pilfered his disintegrating pullover made from blue and red threads.

Casdagli took these precious threads and canvas and began to cross stitch. He ran a textile company before the war broke out, so he knew a bit about sewing. What resulted was an embroidered object closely resembling a sampler, which is still in family hands alongside Casdagli's other embroideries. In its centre is an inscription which reads:

THIS WORK WAS DONE BY MAJOR A.T. CASDAGLI NO. 3311 WHILE IN CAPTIVITY AT DOSSEL-WARBURG GERMANY DECEMBER 1941

The text is written in all caps and all in blue, with the exception of its stitcher's name, which is written in red.

Framing Casdagli's words is a border with a series of swastikas to represent Germany, hammers and sickles to represent the Soviet Union, eagles to represent the US and lions to represent Britain. Around the text and these national symbols, Casdagli stitched a pattern of dots and dashes. Though the pattern seems random, the dots and dashes are actually Morse code. The defiant messages '**God Save The King**' and '**Fuck Hitler**' are hiding in plain sight.

We can assume that Casdagli's German captors never realised the tiny pattern was Morse code, given that they proudly displayed his sampler in the four POW camps in which Casdagli was imprisoned until his release in 1945. Casdagli ran a needlework school for British prisoners in Oflag IV-B, where 40 of them stitched with unravelled jumpers, needles and threads from Red Cross parcels. The prisoners made bookmarks and embroidered letters for family members, adorned with symbols of freedom like butterflies.

Even when the Red Cross materials started arriving, Casdagli still borrowed from his fellow prisoners — the Cretan general gave Casdagli (or had nicked from him, perhaps?) his pyjamas to be taken apart for thread. With this mixture of Red Cross supplies and inmates' clothes, Casdagli painstakingly stitched letters home. His son, Tony, recalled in a 2011 *Guardian* article written by Patrick Barkham that Casdagli sent him a hand-stitched letter when he was 11 years old, part of which reads, '**It is 1,581 days since I saw you last but it will not be long now. Do you remember when I fell down the well? Look after Mummy till I get home again**'. With those pyjamas he also stitched a map of Crete, involving

45,000 stitches and 190 hours of work.

Another embroidered piece is to some extent a map of life in the camp. It shows Room 13, Spangenberg Castle, illustrating inmates' cells, the few lumps of coal they had to keep warm, a sign that says, 'BATH EVERY 14 DAYS', and a menu that reads, 'SOUP, POTATOES, WURST, BREAD, SEMOLINA'. At the bottom is a British flag, which flouted the camp's rule against national flags. Casdagli hid it under a canvas flap that said in German, 'DO NOT OPEN'.

Casdagli was freed in 1945 and flown back to Britain. Once his son Tony retired, the two men began to stitch together. Casdagli stitched for the rest of his life. From his first defiant stitches grew a stitching lineage. ●

Codemakers Codebreakers

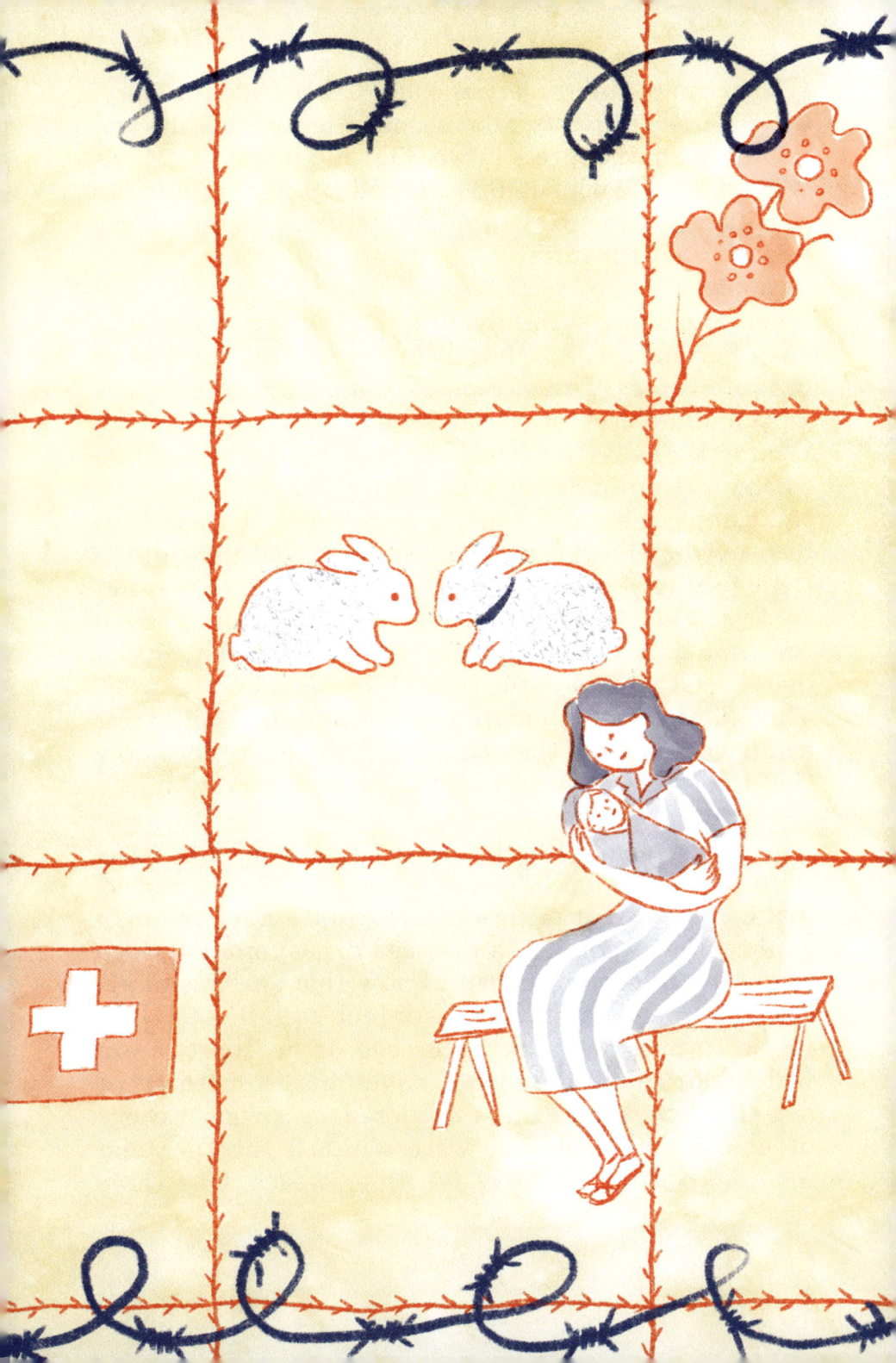

Sometimes, embroidery is code. It was code for Mary, Queen of Scots, who stitched sentiments she was not allowed to express in writing, and it was for Major Alexis Casdagli, who used Morse code to spew profanities at Hitler. For the women of Changi Prison, embroidery was a cipher for survival.

When Singapore surrendered to the Japanese army on 15th February 1942, those who were living there were put into camps. These teachers, doctors, nurses, police, nuns and missionaries from Britain, Australia, Canada, Denmark, the Netherlands and Indonesia were sent to Changi Prison in eastern Singapore. When they got to the camps, men and women were separated and sent into extremely overcrowded camps. Children joined their mothers and boys over the age of 12 were sent to live with the men. They were not allowed to communicate except for during occasional organised meetings that were supervised by Japanese guards. Though the men's camp and women and children's camp were nearby, they could not let each other know that they were alive amidst disease and starvation.

A prisoner named Ethel Mulvany had an idea to solve this communication barrier. She had her fellow prisoners make squares for a patchwork quilt. Each woman could stitch a code — a message or a symbol — into the quilt to let her husband know that she was okay. Each woman was given a six-inch-square of white fabric from a rice sack, flour bag or bedsheet, upon which she embroidered her name and 'something of herself'. The squares, embroidered in a wide variety of colours and stitches, were stitched together and made into three quilts of 66 squares each. The three quilts were made for the Red Cross organisations of Britain, Australia and Japan. The British Changi quilt is in the collection of the British Red Cross, while the Australian and Japanese quilts are in the Australian War Memorial. The Japanese authorities gave the Changi women permission to send their quilts to the military hospital at the Changi barracks. The news that women and children were alive spread from the hospital to other parts of the camps. For some soldiers, the quilts brought the first news that their wives and children had survived.

While the coded meanings of many of the patchwork squares have been lost, some remain: E. Blackman's depiction of a toddler with a curl of hair and wreath on top of their head is likely a depiction of her child, a sign to her husband that they were safe. A depiction of a mother rabbit with a baby rabbit wearing a blue collar indicates that a son was born in the prison. K. Heath's depiction of Changi Prison perhaps illustrated where exactly she was in the camp when she undertook her embroidery, allowing her husband to visualise her despite their separation. Through stitch, using innocent images like flowers, flags, animals and Disney characters, the women of Changi were codemakers and their husbands and sons codebreakers. ●

Many Innocents

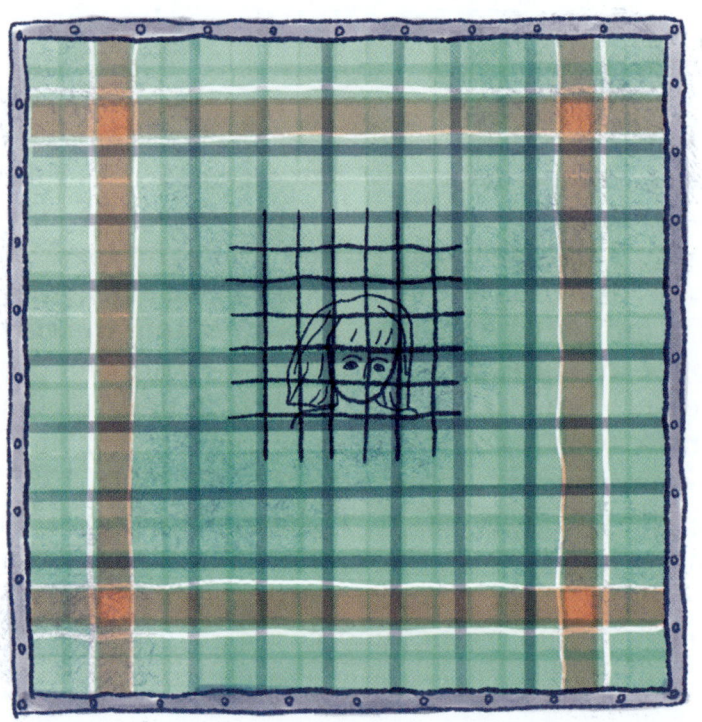

Have Perished

As Major Alexis Casdagli stitched his Morse code sampler border and the prisoners of Changi Prison embroidered upon their rice sack squares, a woman 792 miles away from Dössel-Warburg, Germany and 7,482 miles away from Changi, Singapore also sat in a prison cell, stitching. She embroidered a letter on a handkerchief to commemorate her fellow prisoners and to say goodbye to her family and friends. In the face of certain death, she stitched.

In 1941, Rada Nikolić (1922–1942), a nineteen-year-old worker from Bajina Bašta, Yugoslavia (now Serbia), was arrested and put into the Banjica concentration camp for participating in the anti-fascist organisation the Yugoslav Partisans, also known as the National Liberation Army. She was captured in Bajina Bašta and, in Užice, she was tried by the Nazis and sentenced to death. From there she was taken to the Banjica concentration camp and made to live in the part of the camp occupied by those who were waiting for execution.

While in the camp, Nikolić began to embroider on a multicoloured checked handkerchief made of cotton. Was it her handkerchief, an artefact of her life before internment, or was it another prisoner's? We will likely never know.

In the centre of the handkerchief is a stitched depiction of a girl in a jail cell. I say 'girl' rather than 'woman' because really, that's what she is. She has big eyes, a single line for a nose, and a mouth hidden by bars. She has a defiant brow. She has a fringe and hair that stops at its intersection with her bare shoulders.

The bars behind which her face floats is more a grid, 36 vertical and horizontal lines. This woman, surely Nikolić, embodies a calm confidence, anger, and youth.

Above Nikolić and the bars are several lines of text, written in Bosnian, Croatian, Montenegrin and Serbian (also known as Serbo-Croatian). In English, they read:

> As a memento, to my dear Mommy,
> from her daughter Rada
>
> Greetings to Mommy, Coka, Sava, Toma,
> July 20th
>
> I keep thinking about you
> and waiting for them to take me out
>
> Rada Nikolić, B. Bašta,
> born on August 28, 1922
>
> Arrested on January 1,
> convicted and shot on January 24
>
> Greetings to all dear and beloved your Rada
> July 25th
>
> Don't grieve I'm not the only one,
> many innocents have perished

I am grateful to Serbian artist Milica Dukić, who shared this heartbreaking translation on her blog in 2021.

At the top of the handkerchief is an embroidered list of Nikolić's fellow anti-fascist comrades and the date on which each was executed in Banjica. Even though Nikolić stitched that she was shot on the 24th of January 1942, she stitched a greeting to her family on the 25th of July that year. The only date not included on the handkerchief is Nikolić's own date of execution: the 20th of August 1942. She missed her twentieth birthday by only eight days.

After Nikolić's execution, her friends from the execution camp smuggled it out and gave it to her mother, Milka Nikolić. In 1961, she gave it to the Užice National Museum, where it still resides.

Rada Nikolić is the only embroiderer in this book who depicted herself while imprisoned. With this self-portrait she reaches out to us 80 years later, transcending the walls of the Banjica concentration camp. She puts a face to the often anonymous work of incarceration stitching. ●

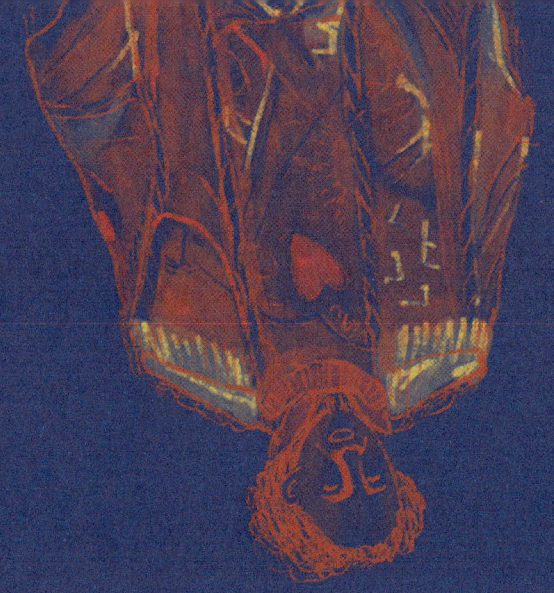

Becoming God

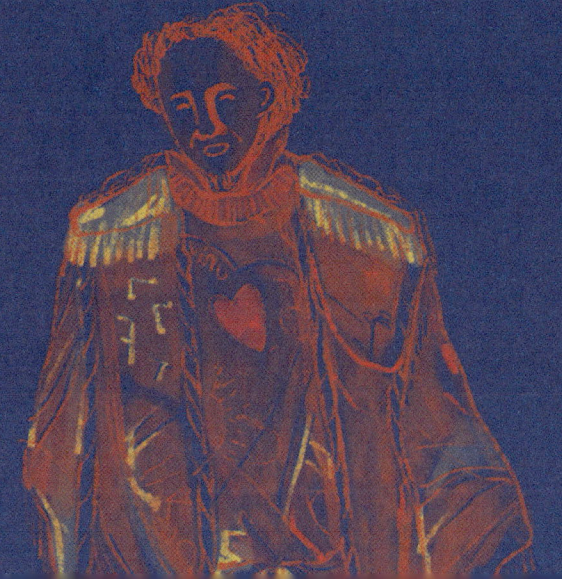

Arthur Bispo do Rosário (1909–1989) thought himself to be Jesus Christ. He did not view himself as an artist, despite making approximately 1,000 works which are now in the collection of Museu Bispo do Rosário Arte Contemporânea. He produced these objects, many of them embroidered, to record reality.

Bispo do Rosário was born in Japaratuba, Brazil, the descendant of African slaves. He was an apprentice sailor in the Brazilian Navy but was discharged for insubordination. He was a boxer, a handyman, an employee of the Light Department of Trams in Rio de Janeiro and an attendant to a wealthy family. On the night of the 22nd of December 1938, Bispo de Rosário was visited by angels. They told him he was Jesus Christ and that it was his job to replicate the entire world in preparation for Judgement Day. Two days after his vision he was arrested, hospitalised and diagnosed with paranoid schizophrenia. He was sent to Hospício Pedro II and then to Colônia Juliano Moreira, a psychiatric institution where he spent the rest of his life (with the exception of the years 1954–1963, when he escaped and got by doing odd jobs and making his art). By 1967 he was using 11 cells in Colônia Juliano Moreira's solitary-confinement wing as a studio and storage space, where it was quieter and therefore easier to hear the voices in his head. From there he created his mixed-media works using materials from around the hospital.

Those familiar with Bispo do Rosário's work consider his 'Annunciation Garment' (*Manto da Apresentação*) his masterpiece. He intended to wear it when he met God.

The garment resembles a poncho and is made from a tan-coloured blanket, upon which he embroidered words, numbers and images from everyday life: a ping pong table and paddle; a gramophone; a globe; one bicycle; two bicycles. Train tracks run all over the garment, bringing your eye on a journey up, down and around. The inside is embroidered with the names of every woman Bispo do Rosário knew, stitched in blue threads taken from the psychiatric hospital's uniforms.

Many of Bispo do Rosário's pieces have embroidery at their heart. He created a number of *estandartes*, embroidered banners. Bispo do Rosário embroidered bed sheets on both sides and focused on a variety of topics, creating a sort of visual encyclopaedia. At a distance some of them look like Lorina Bulwer's embroideries, long and narrow. Like Bulwer, Bispo do Rosário stitched in uppercase with no punctuation to break his stride. Some of his hangings read like the Annunciation Garment's interior, with long lists of names. One example is *Dicionário de Nomes Letra A* ('Dictionary of Names Letter A'), which lists people whose first names began with the letter 'A'. Others include diagrams of battleships, maps of Brazil, national flags and hospital buildings. The bedsheets are laden with a mixture of text and image drawn from newspapers and his own memories, a catalogue of life on earth and his experience of it. Bispo do Rosário's art is the world and the world is his art.

Arthur Bispo do Rosário's works are reminiscent of embroidered samplers, the stitching exercises undertaken by so many embroiderers across centuries and continents. Samplers were frequently used to systematically record and practise the embroidery stitches one learned over the course of their needlework education. Bispo do Rosário's works, with their thorough catalogues of objects and names, are reminiscent of the methodical nature of sampler stitching. But in Bispo do Rosário's case, it was not a stitching encyclopaedia he produced, but an encyclopaedia of his universe. ●

The Mystery of Myrllen

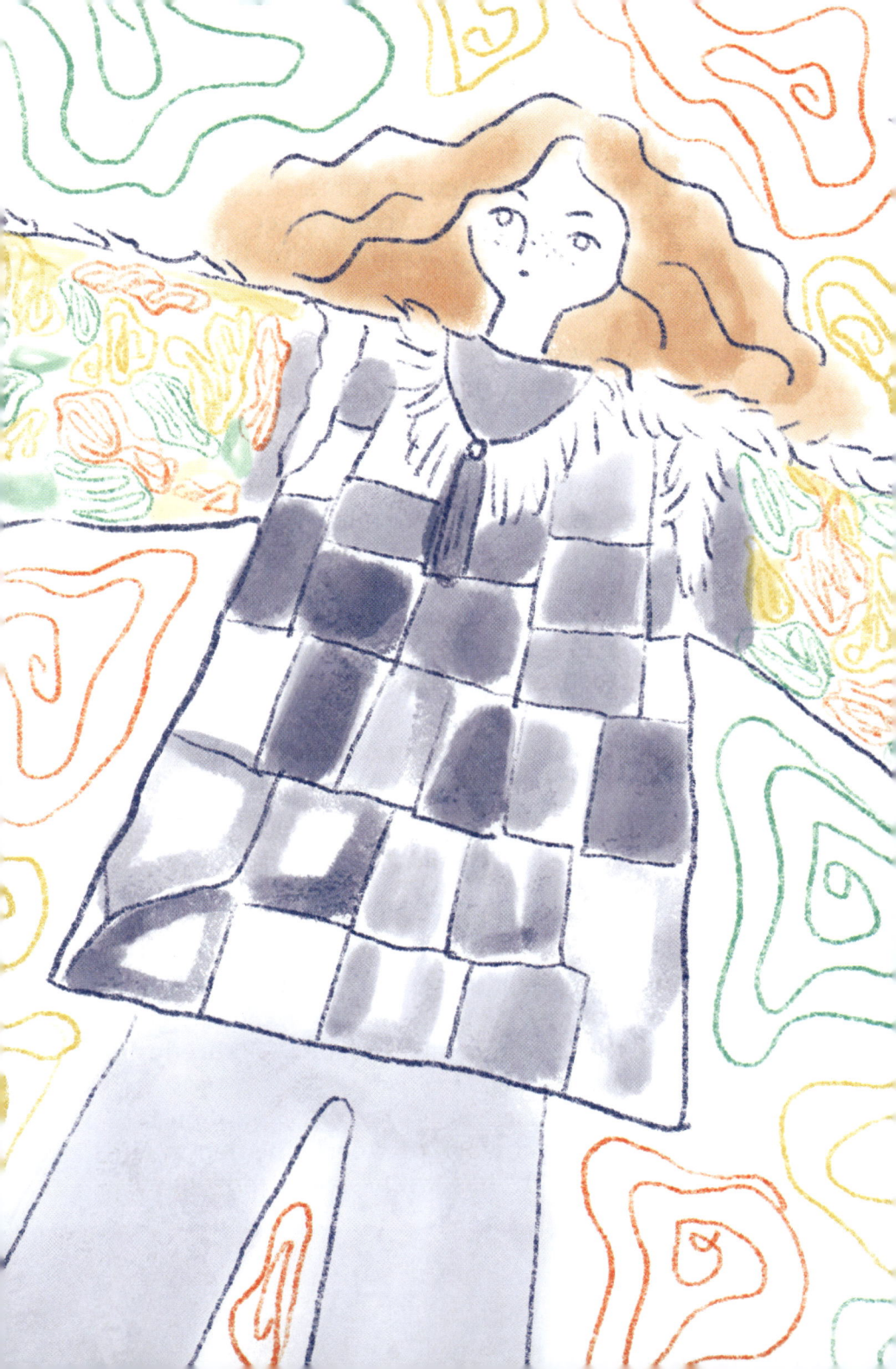

There are three pieces of outerwear discussed in this book. First came Agnes Richter's jacket and Arthur Bispo do Rosário's mantle. We know Richter and Bispo do Rosário's circumstances, their history, and their names. But for this second piece, known as 'Myrllen's Coat', we have nothing but a first name, a pseudonym.

Very little is known about the mysterious 'Myrllen' (c.1920–unknown) who embroidered upon several garments in Knoxville, Tennessee's Eastern State Hospital between 1948 and 1955. Over time, most of her objects and all of her medical records were lost. Myrllen's scarf is on display in Lakeshore Mental Health Center in Knoxville and her coat, the focus here, is in the Tennessee State Museum. The information relayed here comes courtesy of Catherine Heard's article called 'Myrllen's Coat', published in a 2009 issue of The Brock Review.

Almost all we know about Myrllen comes from her nurse Nancy Luttrell. Luttrell met 28-year-old Myrllen, who had red hair and pale skin, when Myrllen was admitted to Eastern State Psychiatric Hospital in 1948. She was admitted straight from jail, where she had been imprisoned for threatening behaviour towards her husband and neighbours. Myrllen was eventually granted a needle and a dull pair of scissors. She received no thread and so, like many others in this book, she took to unravelling the clothing around her — shredding the hospital's laundry rags.

Myrllen's coat is a patchwork of worn blue denim and white cotton sheets. It has wide sleeves edged with white fringe that continues along the coat's back. The sleeves and bottom half of the coat are covered in embroidered figures and text. Even though the top half of the coat's bodice looks unadorned, it is actually covered in wheel stitches worked in various blue threads, stitched so closely together that you can't see the denim underneath. Her stitches go round and round yet are contained, almost like they, too, are stuck in a psychiatric hospital.

Myrllen skilfully used satin, chain and wheel stitches on the coat's bottom half and sleeves to replicate a variety of textures like hair, wood and tree bark. For things that needed a bit of dimensionality, like noses, lips, and eyes, she layered stitches to create a slightly raised surface. It seems that she was reproducing images she had seen in advertisements: scenes of houses, gardens and domestic spaces with smiling girls and women positioned toward the viewer. These figures, which look as if they have been taken from photographs or drawings, have a high level of detail. Myrllen stitched individual eyelashes, red lipstick and nail polish. Her inspiration ranged from cartoons to Christmas cards.

Interspersed with pop culture imagery appear to be scenes from Myrllen's own life and reflections of her feelings. One tableau shows Myrllen's arrest or her appearance before a judge and another shows a faceless figure falling while holding onto a crutch. In between the embroidered vignettes are bands of text, many of which are unintelligible. Many of the words that are legible are the names of places and people.

In 1955, Myrllen was given chlorpromazine. Chlorpormazine was the first antipsychotic medication on the American market and was marketed in 1954 as a 'chemical lobotomy'. On the medication, Myrllen became less violent and much more reclusive. She also completely stopped sewing and embroidering. Eventually, she denied ever having made her garments. Myrllen's bright, flowing and expressive coat was replaced by a sort of chemical straightjacket.

Coats, jackets, mantles. Warmth, comfort, disguise. The garments Agnes Richter, Arthur Bispo do Rosário, and Myrllen embroidered were not just practical in the draughty spaces of psychiatric hospitals. These outerwear garments also allowed them to share their inner thoughts, their outlook and their memories with the outside world. They wore both their heart and their art on their sleeves. For Myrllen, the garment meant to keep her warm was also a reflection on her traumatic past and an idealised, fictitious present she could not access within the hospital's walls. What did she think of the jacket once she forgot that it was the work of her own hands? Perhaps even though she did not know it was her stitching, she knew it contained her story. ●

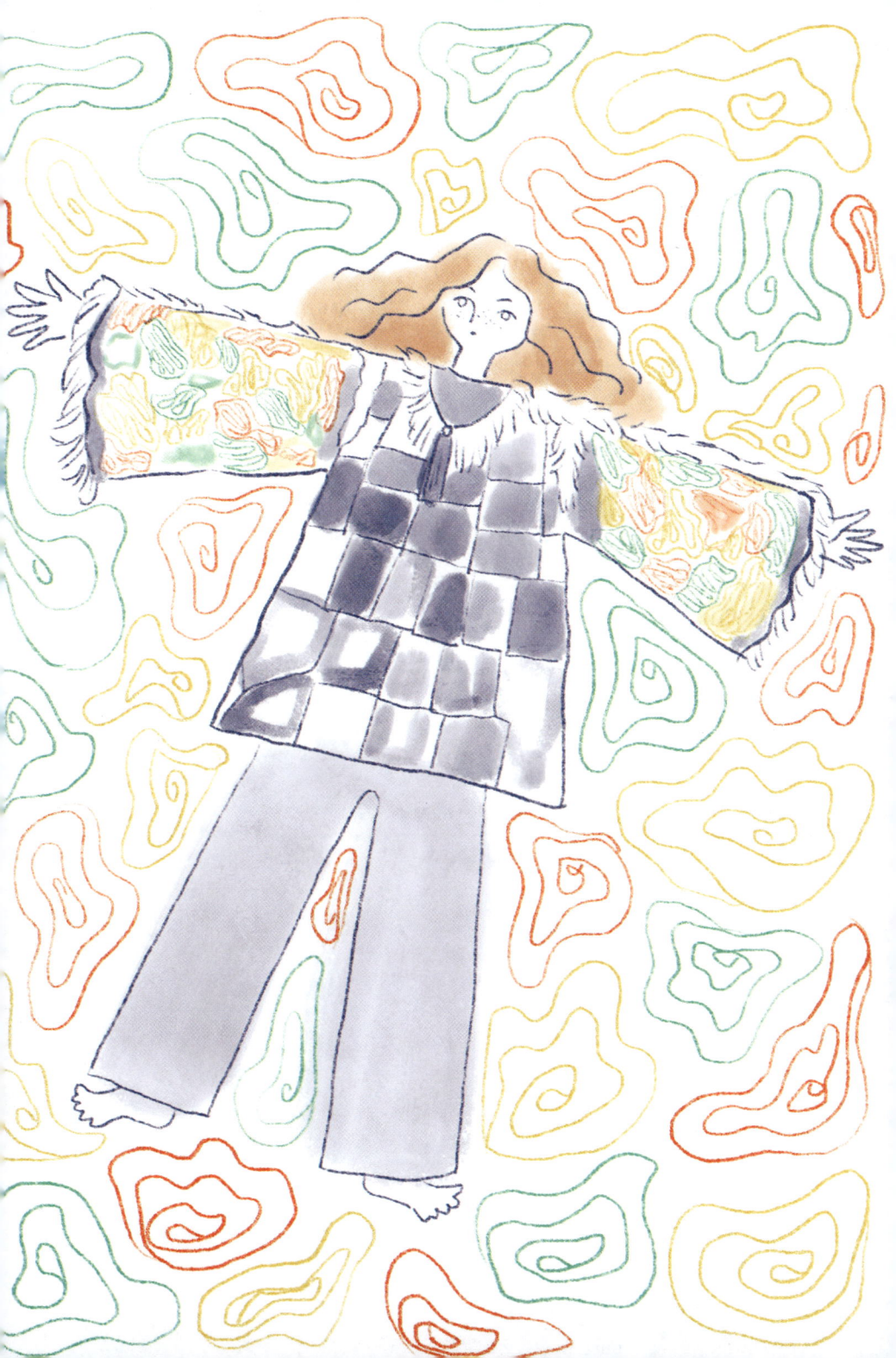

Betsy Ross

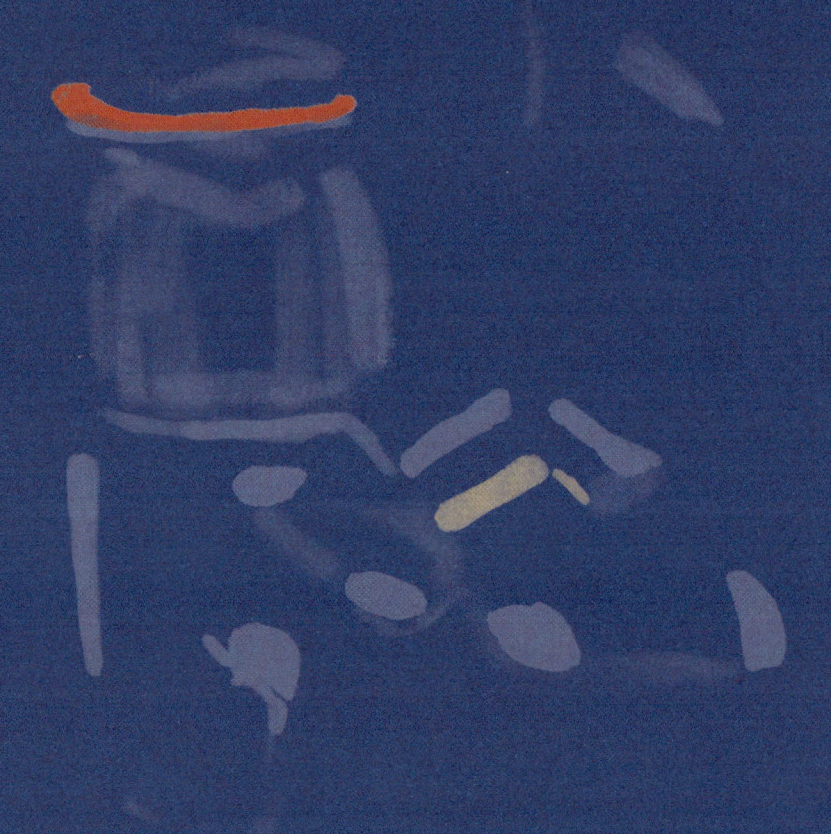

This book has been filled with stories of loss, of despair, of desperation. In a book about stitching in prisons and mental health facilities, that is unfortunately inevitable. But not all embroidery that happens in these places is the stuff of sadness. Stitching also offers autonomy, processing, hope. This final story is about how embroidery in spaces of incarceration does not just trap, it frees.

Ray Materson (1954–), the only living embroiderer in this book, was sentenced to fifteen years in jail for a string of robberies. About a year into a total of eight years he spent in the prison, Materson found himself bored and desperate for something to do. He remembered his grandmother being absorbed in sewing. In a 1994 article in The New York Times ('From scraps of prison cloth a miniature world grows'), Materson told Rita Reif, 'I can still see the red shawl, her tan sewing basket, the balls of floss and the metallic sewing hoops'. It seems this memory paired with the news that his favourite American college football team, University of Michigan, was going to the Rose Bowl. (The Rose Bowl is one of the biggest American college football games of the year, always played on New Year's Day. It is a huge deal.) Materson is a Michigan native, so wanted to do something to show his team pride. Using a sewing needle he borrowed from a prison guard and unravelled socks, he stitched a 'Michigan M' in the team's colours, yellow and blue.

So began Materson's stitching career. He used cotton fabric from boxer shorts and handkerchiefs and made a round stretcher, cutting off the top ring of a plastic jar using a toenail clipper. He embroidered

Harley-Davidson emblems, initials for hats, flags, hearts and flowers for his prison mates, who often sent his embroideries to their loved ones and paid him in cigarettes, bags of coffee and sewing supplies in the form of socks and shoelaces. Materson's fellow inmates gave him the nickname 'Betsy Ross', an American seamstress credited with sewing the first official US flag.

As Materson's skills grew he began to stitch pictures of life inside and outside of prison. He stitched baseball players, family members, childhood memories, scenes from films and famous figures. Most of his pieces are approximately 2 ¼ inches wide by 2 ¾ inches tall (or approximately 5.7 by 7 centimetres) and involve 1,200 stitches per inch.

Materson started gaining attention in the art world even before his release from prison in 1995, his tiny embroideries adorning the walls of the American Primitive Gallery. Even after his release, he never stopped stitching. He has made a career out of stitching, publishing an autobiography called *Sins and Needles: A Story of Spiritual Mending* in 2002 and making art that is included in exhibitions around the world and in the permanent collections of the American Folk Art Museum and American Visionary Art Museum, amongst others. He still uses unravelled socks as his embroidery thread. For Materson, incarceration unexpectedly led to artistic discovery and economic freedom. ●

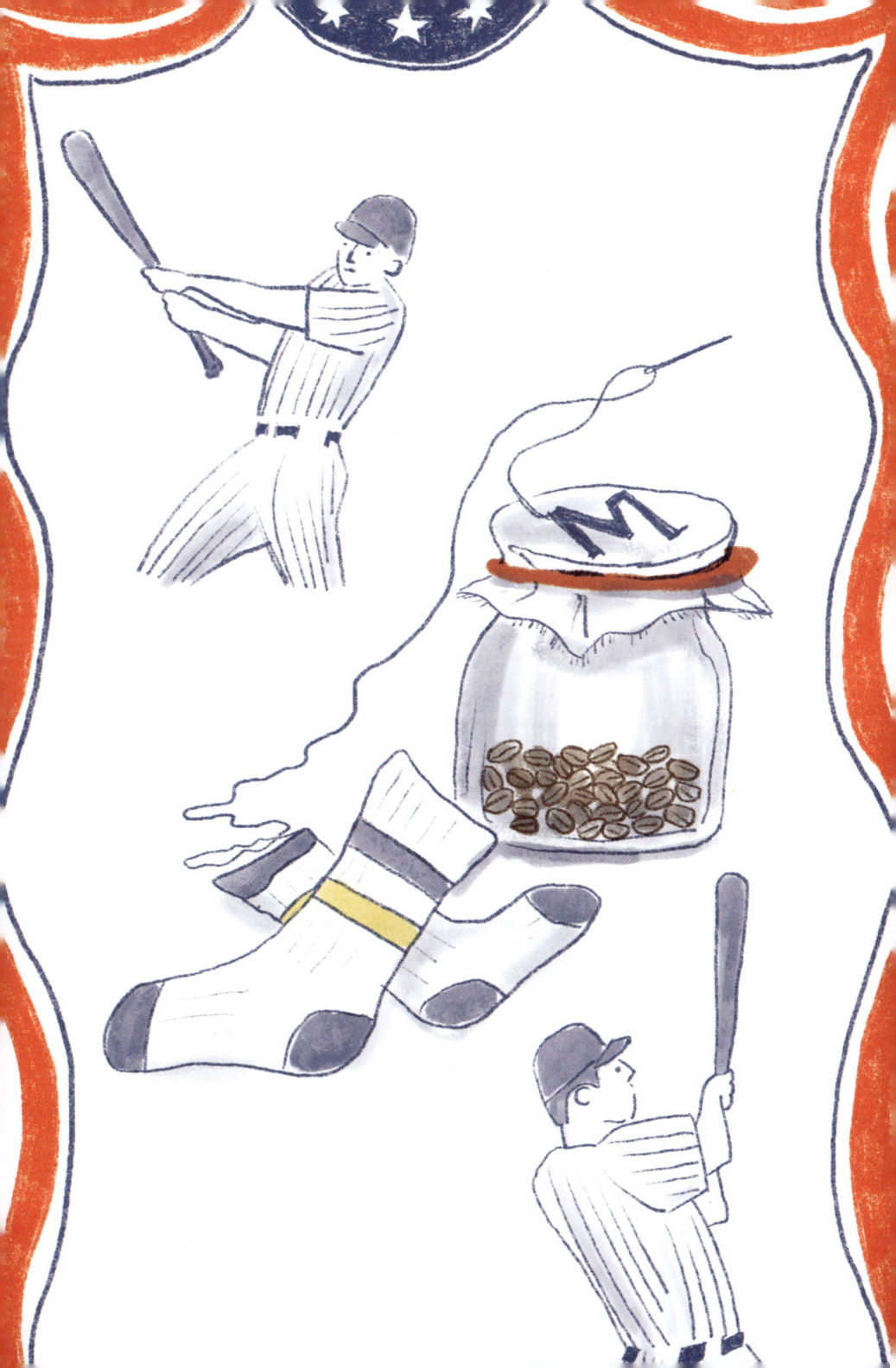

Conclusion

This has not been a happy collection of stories. There has been injustice, violence, force and abuse. Most of the embroiderers profiled here died in prison or in hospital. None of them entered these prisons and mental health facilities willingly. This book, then, is less of a celebration and more of a memorial. Here we remember those who were and still are the victims of carcerality, and push for a dismantling of these systems. Here we memorialise not the gentle, leisured, affluent embroiderer but the unruly, desperate one.

There is rage in these pages. It is Lorina Bulwer's rage toward the brother who pushed her into the Great Yarmouth Workhouse and the system that kept her there, and it is the Suffragettes' fury against a society that could not bear for them to vote. There is frustration, too, felt in Mary, Queen of Scots's missed stitches and Agnes Richter's longing to read. And then there is stoicism, Annie Parker stitching with her own hair verses like, 'Though dark my path and sad my lot / Let me be still and murmur not' and Rada Nikolić's message to her family that reads, 'Don't grieve I'm not the only one, many innocents have perished.'

But in this darkness there are glimmers of light. In Major Alexis Casdagli's butterflies and Ray Materson's successful career, there is hope. And in the symbolism of babies and birds on the Changi quilts and the tattered dress, pecans and a braid of a mother's hair in *Ashley's Sack*, we can find love. In each stitch explored is a longing for a different, more just world.

Isabella Rosner is Curator of the Royal School of Needlework, Research Consultant at Witney Antiques and host of the *Sew What?* podcast.

An art historian who studies material culture from the seventeenth through nineteenth century, Isabella specialises in the study of early modern women's needlework, especially British examples, and schoolgirl samplers across all time periods. She is a 2023 BBC/AHRC New Generation Thinker and recently completed her PhD at King's College London, where she studied Quaker women's needle, shell and wax work before 1800. Isabella frequently lectures and publishes about needlework, textiles, and girlhood.

Author

Takako Copeland is a Japanese illustrator and print maker based in London. She grew up in the Japanese countryside surrounded by nature, which made her especially conscious of the changing seasons and inspires her to create with colour.

After completing a graphic design degree from Central Saint Martins, Takako began working as an illustrator building up images with layers of colour, drawing her towards letterpress and RISO printing techniques.

Her illustrations often focus on characters, domestic scenes and family life and she describes her style as vibrant, joyful and humorous.

Illustrator

Common Threads Press is a small press that specialises in the radical histories of crafts and making.

Established in 2019, we publish books, zines, and curate events that uplift marginalised histories of creative work. Our publications are written collaboratively with early-career researchers, writers, students and academics from all around the world who share our love for craft histories.

Publisher

MORE FROM COMMON THREADS PRESS:

**Stitching the Intifada:
Embroidery and Resistance
in Palestine**
Rachel Dedman
978-1-06862-501-5

**Many Hands Make a Quilt:
Short Histories of
Radical Quilting**
Jess Bailey
978-1-06862-502-2

**Mauka to Makai:
Hawaiian Quilts and the
Ecology of the Islands**
Marenka Thompson-Odlum
978-1-06862-500-8

**Rights Not Charity:
Protest Textiles and
Disability Activism**
Gill Crawshaw
978-1-91632-346-9

**The Norfolk Trans Joy
Community Quilt Zine**
Alice Bigsby-Bye,
Beau Brannick,
Poppy Marriott &
Laura Moseley
978-1-06862-503-9

**Slow Grown:
Plants, Folklore
& Natural Dyeing**
Ciara Callaghan
978-1-39992-032-2

**Diasporic Threads:
Black Women,
Fibre & Textiles**
Sharbreon Plummer
978-1-39991-944-9

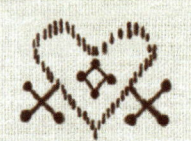